Some Girls Do and Some Girls Don't

Some Girls Do and Some Girls Don't
Sheet Music Covers

Text by Tony Locantro

Quartet Books

London Melbourne New York

First published by Quartet Books Limited 1985
A member of the Namara Group
27/29 Goodge Street, London W1P 1FD

Copyright © 1985 by EMI Music Publishing Ltd

British Library Cataloguing in Publication Data
Some girls do and some girls don't.
1. Music title-pages — Pictorial works
I. Locantro, Tony
769.5   ML112.5

ISBN 0-7043-3456-9

Design Namara Design
Phototypeset by AKM Associates (UK) Limited
Printed in Italy by Sagdos, Brugherio

FOREWORD

The pictorial sheet music cover came into general use in the middle of the nineteenth century. Until then pictorial covers had been rare because they involved the use of engraved copper plates – an expensive process which produced only a small run before the plates wore out – and any colouring would have been done by hand. The introduction of chromo-lithography in 1837, using stones as the printing blocks, made it possible to produce multi-coloured pictures easily, cheaply and in quantities of up to 5000 from each set of stones. This revolutionary process, which coincided with the rise in popularity of the music hall as a medium of mass entertainment, coupled with the growth of interest in the performance of music in the home, meant that the songs and pieces of music performed in the supper rooms, music halls and at concerts could be published and sold in large quantities. The covers were to feature attractive pictures of the performers or topical scenes in striking colours which acted as a further incentive to encourage sales.

Although sheet music covers were originally expected to be ephemeral creations, they have proved to be of interest to later generations and it is now recognized that they provide a fascinating insight into the fashions and styles of past eras. The British music covers from the first flowering of the music hall proper in the 1880s show not only the performers themselves in splendid full-length portraits in costume by accomplished artists such as Alfred Concannon, but also scenes of contemporary life in Victorian times. The American covers from the first quarter of the twentieth century evoke all the brash exuberance and innocent excitement of the ragtime era and the beginning of the jazz age. The Continental covers from the 1920s and 1930s recapture an entirely different feeling of a time of sophistication, indulgence and decadence.

All the English covers are from the archives of EMI Music Publishing Limited, which now controls the catalogues of many of the greatest names in the history of British popular music publishing including Charles Sheard & Company, Francis, Day & Hunter (originally Francis Brothers & Day), Bert Feldman & Company, Herman Darewski Music Publishing Company and Reynolds & Company.

The covers have been chosen solely for their visual merit and there has been no attempt to present a picture of the development of sheet music cover design, to highlight the work of any particular illustrator or to include a representative selection of songwriters or performers. The pictures are there simply to be enjoyed in their own right as superior examples of a simple art-form which has given pleasure to many.

TONY LOCANTRO, 1985

ACKNOWLEDGEMENTS

Special thanks to Dr Robert Kittler for research on the German and Austrian material and to John Whitehorn of EMI Music Publishing Archives.

The Publisher would like to acknowledge Remick and Wiener Boheme for the reproduction of their covers.

BIBLIOGRAPHY

Barker, Tony *A Calendar for 1984* EMI Music Publishing Ltd, 1983.

Beaver, Patrick *The Spice of Life* Elm Tree Books/Hamish Hamilton Ltd, 1979.

Busby, Roy *British Music Hall* Paul Elek Ltd, 1976.

Claghorn, Charles Eugene *Biographical Dictionary of American Music* Parker Publishing Company Inc., 1973.

Fuld, James J. *The Book of World Famous Music* Crown Publishers Inc., 1971.

Gammond, Peter *Music Hall Song Book* David & Charles/EMI Music Publishing Ltd, 1975.

Gammond, Peter *Your Own, Your Very Own!* Ian Allen Ltd, 1971.

Gammond, Peter and Clayton, Peter *A Guide to Popular Music* Phoenix House Ltd, 1960.

Gammond, Peter and Colehan, Barney *The Good Old Days Songbook* British Broadcasting Corporation/EMI Music Publishing Ltd, 1980.

Garrett, John M. *Sixty Years of British Music Hall* Chappell & Co./André Deutsch, 1976.

Haill, Catherine *Victorian Illustrated Music Sheets* H.M. Stationery Office, London 1981.

Hirschhorn, Clive *The Hollywood Musical* Octopus Books Ltd, 1981.

Mander, Raymond and Mitchenson, Joe *British Music Hall* Gentry Books, 1974.

Murrells, Joseph *The Book of Golden Discs* Barrie & Jenkins Ltd, 1974.

Pearsall, Ronald *Victorian Popular Music* David & Charles Ltd, 1973.

Pearsall, Ronald *Victorian Sheet Music Covers* David & Charles Ltd, 1973.

Slonimsky, Nicholas, *Baker's Biographical Dictionary of Musicians* Schirmer Books, 1978.

Spaeth, Sigmund *A History of Popular Music in America* Phoenix House Ltd, 1948.

Wilk, Max *Memory Lane* Studio International Publications Ltd, 1973.

Some Girls Do and Some Girls Don't

'LE CHEVALERESQUE QUADRILLE'

Music by Bohlman

By the middle of the nineteenth century the piano had established itself as the principal medium of home entertainment. The advent in about 1840 of small upright 'cottage' pianos of attractive appearance at prices as low as £10 meant that they were within the reach of a large section of the population, especially the middle classes. The interest in dance music was enormous and, led by the young Queen Victoria herself, the nation was hungry for valses, quadrilles and polkas to dance to at balls and parties or just to play for their own sake as instrumental piano solos in sitting rooms and parlours up and down the country. The firm of Charles Sheard and Company, established in 1846, turned out a series of songs and instrumental pieces under the title of 'Musical Bouquet' to meet the demand for music to be performed in the home. The copies were massproduced relatively cheaply and incorporated the new concept of pictorial designs in place of the old lettering designs, albeit somewhat tentatively in that the picture occupied only the upper part of the cover.

LE CHEVALERESQUE QUADRILLE.

ARRIVÉE DES CHEVALIERS AU CAROUSEL.

'LA PETITE COQUETTE QUADRILLE'

Music by C. Schubert

This quadrille is another early example of a 'Musical Bouquet' publication. The quadrille was a square dance of French origin with five figures danced usually by four couples, or sometimes other numbers. The separate sections that made up the figures could either be especially composed or adapted from existing melodies from popular songs, folk music, operas, ballets or other stage works. In this particular case the music was written for the quadrille by C. Schubert and the names of the five figures are 'Pantalon', 'Eté', 'Poule', 'Pastourelle' and 'Finale'. The interest in the quadrille, as well as the equally popular valse and polka, can be partly attributed to the activities of Louis Antoine Jullien, the French conductor and composer. He began presenting orchestral concerts in London in 1840, which were aimed at bringing good music cheaply to a wide public. His programmes were generally arranged for huge numbers of performers and consisted of works by composers such as Mozart, Haydn and Beethoven, together with quadrilles and polkas of his own devising. The concerts were given in places like the Zoological Gardens and Surrey Gardens, as well as at more conventional venues such as the Drury Lane and Covent Garden Theatres. They were a spectacular success and Jullien soon set up a company to publish his own works for home performance as piano solos and duets.

LA PETITE COQUETTE QUADRILLE _ C. SCHUBERT.

No 1.

PANTALON

'THE ZULEIKA AND THE EMMELINE POLKAS'

Music by Wély

The polka was the most popular of the dances fashionable in the Victorian era, to an extent that can be described as 'polkamania'. On this publication there is a note by Mrs N. Henderson on the origin of the polka together with instructions on how to dance it. Mrs Henderson goes on to give the following advice:

Ladies, not being all alike, either in figure or facility of movement, should consider well whether or not they are imposing a severe task on their partners by their impassiveness, and generally assist them when they seem to require it. A Lady who dances well can easily do this and however ponderous in person may make herself as light, in the arms of a partner, as a slender girl of eighteen. Many ladies of magnitude however object to do this and play the passive young girls, and thus convert a light and agreeable pastime into a task of extreme toil and hardship to the gentlemen who dance with them. The gallantry of the gentlemen seldom makes more of this than material for an innocent joke, but even this may very easily be avoided by a little more activity on the part of the lady. It is all very well for slender young ladies to be led; but a woman of mature figure and stately appearance aspires to lead, and the leadership becomes her when dancing with *boys*, even though the boys be *old ones*. All romping, dragging, hugging and leaning or stooping over the shoulders of partners are decidedly objectionable; in respectable houses they are universally discouraged. Every accomplishment has its vulgarities, and so has the Polka. But a person of refined taste can at once perceive the difference between the elegant and the inelegant, the delicate and the indelicate.

THE ZULEIKA & THE EMMELINE POLKAS.

COMPOSED BY WÉLY.

Nᵒ 244.

V. S.

INSTRUCTIONS FOR DANCING THE POLKA.

The origin of the Polka is unknown, but it is generally believed to be an ancient Scythian dance, as it has bee
immemorially known and practised in the Northern countries of Europe, namely, Russia, Servia, Bohemia, Germany and

'I'LL BET YOU A DOLLAR YOU DON'T'

Composed and sung by Sam Redfern; lyrics by J. Haydon; published March, 1877

Sam Redfern (1855–1915) worked in the music halls under the curious appellation of 'The Black Boss of the Benighted Bohemians' and wore black-face makeup although his songs were not in the negro idiom usually used by the other 'black-face' entertainers. G.H. Chirgwin (1854–1922) was a contemporary of Redfern's, who also made a speciality of working in black-face, but with the eccentric variation of leaving a large white diamond around one eye. He was known as 'The White-Eyed Kaffir' and was said to have been influenced by Sam Redfern in his early days.

I'LL BET YOU A DOLLAR YOU DON'T.

1275.

Does anyone know what I'm to going to say? I'll bet you a dollar you don't.
If I lose the wager, will anyone pay? I'll bet you a dollar you don't.

ENT. STA. HALL.

PRICE,

COMPOSED & SUNG BY

SAM. REDFERN.

WRITTEN EXPRESSLY FOR HIM BY

J. HAYDON.

LONDON.

FRANCIS BROS AND DAY (BLENHEIM HOUSE) 351 OXFORD ST W

PUBLISHERS OF

'THE MARQUIS OF CAMBERWELL GREEN'

Music by E.R. Shrosberry; lyrics by Harry Boden;

sung by T.W. Barrett;

published May, 1884

T.W. Barrett (1851–1935) was known on the halls as 'A Nobleman's Son'. He took this appellation from one of his songs, not from his father who was a shoemaker in Birmingham. Barrett was a comedian with a laconic style whose songs included 'I've Been and Got Married Today', 'I Don't Like London' and 'Jolly as a Sand Boy'. In 'The Marquis of Camberwell Green' Barrett portrays a 'masher' whose night-time activities as a would-be man-about-town – albeit arrayed in cheap finery – are a far cry from his daytime occupation as a tripe dresser and a trusser of fowls. The song is typical of many of the period and echoes the ambitions of most of the music hall audience to escape at night from their unglamorous daytime jobs and ape the 'toffs' and 'swells' of society.

THE MARQUIS OF CAMBERWELL GREEN.

1884.

WRITTEN BY

HARRY BODEN.

COMPOSED BY

E. R. SHROSBERRY.

SUNG WITH IMMENSE SUCCESS BY

T. W. BARRETT.

LONDON
FRANCIS BROS AND DAY, (BLENHEIM HOUSE,) OXFORD ST W.
PUBLISHERS OF,
Smallwoods Pianoforte Tutor,(The Universal Favorite,) The Mohawk Minstrels Magazine, &c &c.
Tho' Packer Lith.

ENT. STA. HALL

PRICE, 3/

'SOME GIRLS DO AND SOME GIRLS DON'T'

Music by W.G. Eaton; lyrics by T.S. Lonsdale;

sung by Arthur Roberts;

published May, 1877

Arthur Roberts (1852–1933) was an important figure in the music hall who made the transition to operetta. He is credited with being one of the originators of the form that came to be known as musical comedy. In the 1870s he played the halls as a well-dressed man-about-town and, in spite of the risqué nature of his material, he soon established himself as a top act. He left the music halls in 1883 to pursue a more 'legitimate' career and became a successful burlesque comedian in opera bouffe. In 1891 he starred in the musical farce *In Town*, presented by George Edwardes at the Prince of Wales Theatre. This is now regarded as the first musical comedy. After further musical shows Roberts returned to variety in 1904 at the Empire, Leicester Square, with a revival of his earlier music hall hit 'Some Girls Do and Some Girls Don't', whose double entendres had evidently lost none of their spice. The writers of the song, T.S. Lonsdale and W.G. Eaton, were regular contributors to the music hall and their songs include 'This is the House that Jerry Built' (1885) sung by James Fawn and 'My Aesthetic Love' (1881) sung by The Great Vance. The popular audience participation number 'Oh, the Fairies' (1879) was later taken up as a regular anthem of the Players Theatre, London, where music hall in its traditional form is still played today.

1064.

SOME GIRLS DO AND SOME GIRLS DON'T

COMPOSED BY

W. G. EATON.

ENT. STA. HALL.

WRITTEN BY

T. S. LONSDALE.

AUTHOR OF "TOMMY MAKE ROOM FOR YOUR UNCLE."
SUNG WITH IMMENSE SUCCESS BY

PRICE. 3/-

ARTHUR ROBERTS

LONDON.
FRANCIS BROS AND DAY (BLENHEIM HOUSE) 351 OXFORD ST W
PUBLISHERS OF
Smallwood's Pianoforte Tutor, the Easiest to Teach and to Learn from

'THE FLIPPITY FLOP YOUNG MAN'

Music by E. Jonghmans; lyrics by Harry Adams;
sung by Charles Godfrey;
published 1882

Charles Godfrey (1851–1900) achieved his biggest successes in patriotic flag-waving dramatic sketches in which he portrayed Nelson, Wellington, Drake and Gordon, accompanied by appropriate music and cannon-fire effects. His repertoire ranged from comic numbers like 'The Masher King', 'Hi-Tiddly-Hi-Ti' and 'Hold on, Johnny, Hold On, Jack' to melancholy songs about suicide such as 'Across the Bridge' and 'The Lost Daughter'.

In 1881 W.S. Gilbert had satirized the aesthetic movement and Oscar Wilde in particular, who epitomized it in the eyes of the general public, in his comic opera *Patience* in which the central character is a poet called Reginald Bunthorne. Written the following year, 'The Flippity Flop Young Man' uses almost the same words and metre as one of Bunthorne's songs to run through the litany of characteristics of an aesthete, but in this case there is no concealment and explicit references are made to both Oscar Wilde and to *Patience*. The closeness of the parody can be seen from a direct comparison between Adams and Gilbert in the following lines:

W.S. Gilbert	Harry Adams
A most intense young man,	*I'm a very aesthetic young man*
A soulful-eyed young man;	*A non-energetic young man;*
An ultra-poetical, super-aesthetical,	*Slippity, sloppity over the shoppity,*
Out-of-the-way young man.	*Flippity flop young man.*

The copyright in the song was bought outright by Francis Brothers and Day for £19 along with two other works.

2ND EDITION WITH ADDITIONAL VERSES.

16832

THE FLIPPITY FLOP YOUNG MAN

WRITTEN BY

HARRY ADAMS.

COMPOSED BY

E. JONGHMANS.

SUNG WITH IMMENSE SUCCESS BY

CHARLES GODFREY.

ENT. STA. HALL.

FRANCIS, DAY & HUNTER
142, Charing Cross
OXFORD STREET E.C.

LONDON, FRANCIS BROS. & DAY. (BLENHEIM HOUSE) 195, OXFORD ST W.
PUBLISHERS OF SMALLWOODS PIANOFORTE TUTOR. THE EASIEST TO TEACH AND TO LEARN FROM.

'LET GO THE ANCHOR BOYS'

Music and lyrics by Joseph Tabrar; sung by Henri Clark; published November, 1882

Joseph Tabrar (1857–1931) contributed much material to the music hall. He could write a song to order in an hour and claimed to be able to outwrite anyone, including Sullivan and Wagner! His own estimate of his total output was 10,000 songs of which the most lasting is undoubtedly 'Daddy Wouldn't Buy Me a Bow Wow', written in 1893 for Vesta Victoria. His activities ranged through writing jokes, sketches and monologues to plays and pantomime books. He also ran a flourishing business from his own shop in London's York Road, near Waterloo Bridge.

This song is a typical example of Tabrar's facility for the simple but catchy style that brought him success. It relates the way a couple of very nervous lovers over-react when confronted with minor misadventures in watery situations, such as rowing in the River Lea or lunching on a Thames boat at Kew. After Tabrar's death, his heirs sold all the rights in his songs to Francis, Day and Hunter in February 1932 for a lump sum in lieu of the copyright royalties, which would otherwise have continued until 1981. Henri Clark, who performed the song, started as a legitimate actor but took up music hall to exploit his talent for characterization. His gallery of creations included 'The Barber', 'The Waiter' and 'The Mad Butcher', but the most memorable of his numbers is 'She Does the Fandango All Over the Place', which was written by G.W. Hunt in 1883 and is still given the occasional performance in music hall revivals.

LET GO THE ANCHOR BOYS

WRITTEN & COMPOSED BY

J. TABRAR

SUNG WITH IMMENSE SUCCESS
BY

HENRI CLARK.

LONDON.

FRANCIS BROS AND DAY, BLENHEIM HOUSE, OXFORD ST W.

PUBLISHERS OF
Smallwoods Pianoforte Tutor, (The Universal Favorite), The Mohawk Minstrels Magazine &c &c

Thos PACKER LITH

ENT. STA. HALL.

PRICE, 3/

1739.

'NOW YOU'RE MARRIED I WISH YOU JOY'

Music by Hugh Clendon; lyrics by Harry Nichols;

sung by Herbert Campbell;

published June, 1881

Herbert Campbell (1846–1904) was a big star in more than one sense, being of large stature and weighing around nineteen stone. He began his career in a black-face minstrel troupe, but soon found that he could succeed as a solo performer. He eventually discovered that his performances in drag brought him his greatest successes. From the music halls he graduated to pantomime, where for the rest of his life he played the dame, often opposite the great Dan Leno (1860–1904). The music hall songs that he sang dressed as a female of homely aspect included 'At My Time of Life' by T.W. Connor, which poked fun at the women's liberation movement of the 1870s, and 'In My Fust 'Usband's Time' (1882) by Harry Nicholls which told of an old woman yearning for the days gone by.

'Now You're Married I Wish You Joy' (1881) was sung by Campbell in the character of a disillusioned husband who gets no sleep because of the screaming of the babies through the cold winter's nights. He longs for the freedom of his unmarried youth as he listens to his wife singing 'in the most satirical manner' the words of the song he himself used to sing as a child, little knowing what the reality would be!

Now you are married I wish you joy,
First a girl and then a boy.
Seven years after son and daughter,
Pray young couple, kiss together.

NOW YOU'RE MARRIED I WISH YOU JOY.

Wm Spalding Lith

ENT. STA. HALL.

PRICE, 4/.

WRITTEN BY
HARRY NICHOLLS,

COMPOSED BY
HUGH CLENDON,

SUNG WITH IMMENSE SUCCESS BY

HERBERT CAMPBELL.

FRANCIS BROS. & DAY, BLENHEIM HOUSE, OXFORD ST. W.

T PACKER LITH

'JOHN THE MASHER'

Music and lyrics by Marcus Boyle; sung by T.W. Barrett; published September, 1882

Another song, like 'The Marquis of Camberwell Green' (which was also sung by T.W. Barrett) about a 'masher' who tries to impress the ladies with his would-be fine clothes and smart accessories but with quite inadequate financial means. He sports a sixpenny eyeglass and a 'German silver watch' which actually comes from Birmingham and cost 'fifteen bob' (seventy-five pence), a paltry sum compared with the cost of the real thing.

ALSO SUNG BY MR HARRY FORSTER.

JOHN THE MASHER

1716.

WRITTEN & COMPOSED BY

MARCUS BOYLE,

SUNG WITH IMMENSE SUCCESS
BY

T. W. BARRETT.

Pr. 3/-

ENT. STA. HALL.

LONDON: FRANCIS BROS & DAY, (BLENHEIM HOUSE) 195, OXFORD ST. W.
PUBLISHERS OF SMALLWOOD'S PIANOFORTE TUTOR, THE EASIEST TO TEACH & TO LEARN FROM.
STANNARD & SON.

'OH LOR, OH LOR! OH DEAR, OH DEAR!'

A cynical song by Frank W. Green and Oswald Allen;

music by Edmund Forman;

published September, 1881

The cover illustration of this song, drawn in 1881, is an excellent example of the work of Alfred Concannon (1835–86), the best of the cover artists of popular songs during the 1870s and 1880s. Born in London of Irish parents, he began his career as a newspaper illustrator but soon became a freelance artist working on books, posters and music covers where his talent blossomed. His illustrations of songs fall into two distinct categories: full-length portraits of the music hall artists in the costumes or characters in which they performed the songs, and lively scenes illustrating the songs themselves. This is a good example of the latter, full of delicious details like the portrait of the surly vestry clerk on the wall, the notice of a penny refund on the bottle and the leaping cat, no doubt startled by the cries of 'Oh lor, Oh dear' uttered by the two women as they bemoan the woes of the day reported in the newspapers. The song is a typical one and refers, among other things, to the aesthetic movement, nihilists, the Sunday Observance Society, tourists and the continuing troubles in Ireland!

WRITTEN EXPRESSLY FOR THE COMING PANTOMIMES.

OH LOR, OH LOR! OH DEAR, OH DEAR!

A CYNICAL SONG BY

FRANK W. GREEN & OSWALD ALLAN.

MUSIC BY

EDMUND FORMAN.

LONDON: FRANCIS BROS & DAY, (BLENHEIM HOUSE,) 195, OXFORD ST W.
PUBLISHERS OF SMALLWOOD'S PIANOFORTE TUTOR; THE EASIEST TO LEARN & TO TEACH FROM.

Pr. 3/-

Number Twelve

'I WON THE BICYCLE'

Music and lyrics by A.R. Marshall; sung by Harry Randall;
published March, 1884

Harry Randall (1860–1932) was a Londoner who achieved early success on the music hall stage in comedy character songs, sometimes dressed as a woman. He later became a top pantomime dame, succeeding Herbert Campbell and Dan Leno in the prestigious Drury Lane pantomimes between 1904 and 1910. One of Randall's most successful songs was the highly topical 'Who Killed Cock Robin?' which he introduced in 1888. This was the year that the unpopular Commissioner of Police, Sir Charles Warren, whose ineffective methods of trying to catch Jack the Ripper were already causing public disquiet, was forced to resign after his clumsy and brutal handling of a demonstration by the unemployed in Trafalgar Square.

The song 'I Won the Bicycle' tells of a man who won a bicycle in a raffle at his local pub. But, when he went out for a ride with his friend who had also just acquired a bicycle, the pair could not resist stopping for a drink at every pub along the way, with the inevitable result depicted on the cover!

I WON THE BICYCLE.

1860.

WRITTEN & COMPOSED BY

A · R · MARSHALL,

SUNG WITH IMMENSE SUCCESS BY

HARRY RANDALL.

ENT. STA. HALL.

Price 3/=

LONDON: FRANCIS BROS & DAY (BLENHEIM HOUSE,) 195 OXFORD ST. W.
PUBLISHERS OF SMALLWOOD'S PIANOFORTE TUTOR; THE EASIEST TO TEACH, AND TO LEARN FROM.

STANHARD & SON. IMPT

'PEG-LEG POLLY'

Music by G.D. Fox; lyrics by Harry Hunter;

sung by Wil Parker and also T.W. Barrett;

published December, 1883

This lively drawing by Alfred Concannon evokes a vivid picture, very much along the lines of some of the antecedents of the music hall fifty or so years earlier. In those days the clientele was male and gathered in the assembly rooms of various pubs to enjoy convivial musical entertainment, usually of a bawdy nature, adopting the names of glee clubs or harmonic societies to give themselves a cloak of respectability. Places such as the Coal Hole in the Strand, the Cyder Cellars in Maiden Lane and Evans Song and Supper Rooms in Covent Garden were the precursors of the later more respectable saloons and halls where working men brought their wives to enjoy food, drink and entertainment. Later still were the purpose-built music halls which flourished in the late Victorian and Edwardian eras and which the fashionable middle classes, and even on occasion royalty itself, patronized.

The song tells of a particularly unattractive woman, the eponymous Peg-Leg Polly, who makes her husband's life a misery by following him wherever he goes to seek enjoyment and hauling him back home. The words paint a fearsome portrait of the formidable wife:

She's a falsetto voice and a false set of teeth
And a glass eye and a hump.
And a timber peg instead of a leg
And goes with a stump, stump, stump.

SUNG BY MR WILL PARKER.

PEG-LEG POLLY

1876.

WRITTEN BY **HARRY HUNTER.** ALSO SUNG WITH IMMENSE SUCCESS BY **T. W. BARRETT.** COMPOSED BY **G. D. FOX.** Pr. 3/-

ENT. STA. HALL.

LONDON: FRANCIS BROS. & DAY, (BLENHEIM HOUSE) 195, OXFORD ST. W.
PUBLISHERS OF SMALLWOOD'S PIANOFORTE TUTOR, THE EASIEST TO TEACH AND TO LEARN FROM.

'I SAY CABBY!'

Music and lyrics by Joseph Tabrar; sung by George Leybourne; published July, 1881

George Leybourne (1842–84) was one of the greatest stars of the Victorian music hall and was dubbed the *'Lion Comique'*, a name which became generic to this type of performer. Leybourne was tall, strikingly handsome and was always immaculately dressed for his songs, which were usually about 'mashers', 'dandies' or 'heavy swells'. With his melodious voice he also sang sentimental ballads to great effect. During his short but spectacular career he had many good songs, often topical, such as 'Up in a Balloon' of 1868 to celebrate the current craze for ballooning; 'The Daring Young Man on the Flying Trapeze', also in 1868, marking the sensational London season of the French acrobat Léotard; and, best of all, 'Champagne Charlie' which extolled the virtues of 'fizz' so persuasively that the champagne company Moët and Chandon kept him supplied with generous quantities of the beverage, a fact which undoubtedly hastened his early death at the age of forty-two.

Leybourne and his other great music hall contemporaries, Macdermott and Vance, became through their topical songs the spokesmen of the people on matters of the day; in their time the music hall became a medium for contemporary social comment, a fact not always liked by the politicians and the establishment. The popularity of the *Lions Comiques* was so great and their influence over their admiring audience so strong that the Lord Chamberlain was powerless to curb them, even when their songs criticized the police or challenged other forms of authority, including Parliament itself. This song, 'I Say Cabby!' by the prolific music hall writer, Joseph Tabrar, was written in 1881, and is one of Leybourne's typical 'masher' songs which he would have performed in his stylish manner, with many a wink and knowing look, to make it far more vivid in performance than on the written sheet.

I SAY CABBY!

1611.

WRITTEN & COMPOSED
BY
JOSEPH TABRAR.

SUNG WITH THE GREATEST SUCCESS
BY
GEORGE LEYBOURNE.

ENT. STA. HALL.

Pr. 3/.

LONDON: FRANCIS BROTHERS & DAY, BLENHEIM HOUSE, OXFORD ST. W.

'RIDING ON THE TOP OF AN OMNIBUS'

Written, composed and sung by G.W. Hunter;

published October, 1885

This song is an amusing recital of the domestic goings-on seen by a passenger on the top of an omnibus looking into the windows of the houses along the route. The sights include a wife flirting with the lodger, an angry woman chasing her husband with a broom, an aged bachelor trying to sew his trousers with a nail and a little woman waiting for her husband to come home to his tea while he is in a house around the corner with another fellow's wife upon his knee. In Alfred Concannon's witty cover illustration, which expertly captures the spirit of the song, notice the prominent advertisement for the Mohawk Minstrels, the company run by the Francis Brothers and from which their music publishing company sprang. The writer and performer of the song, G.W. Hunter was billed as 'The Mark Twain of the Music Halls' and followed in the tradition of the original *Lions Comiques*, namely Leybourne, Vance and Macdermott.

RIDING ON THE TOP OF AN OMNIBUS

2032

WRITTEN, COMPOSED, & SUNG BY

G. W. HUNTER.

Pr. 3/-

LONDON: FRANCIS BROS. & DAY, (BLENHEIM HOUSE) 195 OXFORD ST W.

PUBLISHERS OF SMALLWOOD'S PIANOFORTE TUTOR THE EASIEST TO TEACH AND TO LEARN FROM

ENT. STA. HALL

Number Sixteen

'MAY GARLAND'

Schottische by W. Smallwood;

published March, 1879

In 1878, just one year after the music publishing company of Francis Brothers and Day had opened its doors, an enterprising organist and music teacher from Kendal called William Smallwood (1831–97) produced for the company a piano tutor. It turned out to be one of the firm's biggest commercial successes and has been in print ever since. 'May Garland' is an instrumental solo written as a Schottische, a slower version of the polka.

May Garland

Schottische
BY
W. Smallwood.

LONDON:
FRANCIS BROS AND DAY (BLENHEIM HOUSE) 351 OXFORD ST W
PUBLISHERS OF
Smallwood's Pianoforte Tutor the Easiest to Teach and to Learn from
T. PACKER LITH & IMP.

ENT. STA. HALL

Solo, 3/-
Duet, 4/-
Septett, 1/-
Full Orchestra 1/6.

1259.

'OLIVE'

Schottische composed by A. Bonser; arranged by C.H.R. Marriott;

published December, 1881

This illustration, which could have served any number of instrumental pieces with equally innocuous titles, bears the signature of William Spalding. He was not in fact an artist, but the proprietor of a studio that employed various craftsmen and designers. They produced many cover designs in a range of styles but they were not individually credited.

OLIVE

SCHOTTISCHE

W. Spalding del?

COMPOSED BY

A. BONSER,

ARRANGED BY

C. M. R. MARRIOTT.

LONDON.

FRANCIS BROS and DAY, BLENHEIM HOUSE, OXFORD ST. W

PUBLISHERS OF

Smallwoods Pianoforte Tutor, (The Universal Favorite), The Mohawk Minstrels Magazine, &c, &c

Thos Packer Lith

ENT. STA. HALL

PRICE, 3/.

1637.

Number Eighteen

'APRIL SHOWERS'

Valse by Warwick Williams;

published January, 1887

This is a simple piano solo in the tradition of the easy salon pieces that were so popular in Victorian times, written by the Musical Director of the Mohawk Minstrels, Warwick Williams.

'MEADOW FLOWERS'

Valse by John James

Another salon piece of a mildly descriptive nature. These short works required little technical skill and could be performed by any pianist with a basic keyboard talent.

'SOMEONE TO SAY GOOD BYE TO'

Music by David Day; lyrics by Harry Hunter;

sung by J. Fuller of the Mohawk Minstrels;

published December, 1881

When the brothers James and William Francis decided in 1877 to open a music publishing business to capitalize on the popularity of the songs being written and performed by their Mohawk Minstrel Troupe, they took into partnership as business manager David Day, who had been working for the publishing firm of Hopwood & Crew. The chief lyric writer of the Mohawk Minstrel songs was Harry Hunter, who later joined the company on the death of James Francis in 1886 when the name of the company was changed to Francis, Day & Hunter. Although David Day was primarily a businessman, and a very good one, he also wrote the music to an occasional song such as this one on which he collaborated with Harry Hunter. With the performer credited as J. Fuller of the Mohawk Minstrels, this is an example of the complete tie-up between the elements that formed the chain of success for the Mohawk Minstrels, Harry Hunter and Francis Brothers and Day.

SOMEONE TO SAY GOOD BYE TO.
(DOWN IN THE OLD GREEN LANE)

WRITTEN BY
HARRY HUNTER.

COMPOSED BY
DAVID DAY.

SUNG BY MR J. FULLER. OF THE
MOHAWK MINSTRELS
(AGRICULTURAL HALL, LONDON.)

LONDON.
FRANCIS BROS AND DAY; BLENHEIM HOUSE, OXFORD ST. W

PUBLISHERS OF
Smallwoods Pianoforte Tutor, (The Universal Favorite), The Mohawk Minstrels Magazine &c &c

Thos PACKER LITH

STA. HALL.

Price 3/-
BAND PARTS (for 1st & 2nd Violin
Flute Cornet & Bass complete) 2/6 net
SINGLE PARTS 8d EACH

'OVER THE GARDEN WALL'

Polka arranged by Warwick Williams;

published 1881

Warwick Williams, the Musical Director of the Mohawk Minstrels, wrote and arranged many pieces of music for performance by the Minstrel Troupe and for publication by Francis Brothers and Day. During the course of 1881, Williams also produced several different quadrilles with the title 'Over the Garden Wall' and a polka as well, all of which drew on the song of the same name, by G.D. Fox and Harry Hunter, that appeared in January of that year.

OVER THE GARDEN WALL.

POLKA,
BY
WARWICK WILLIAMS.

LONDON: FRANCIS BROTHER & DAY, BLENHEIM HOUSE, OXFORD St. W.

PRICE ... 4/
MILITARY & BRASS Bᵈ 2/6 NETT
STRING BAND 1/6 "
SEPT ETT 1/ "

'OVER THE GARDEN WALL'

Valse on popular melodies arranged by Charles Godfrey;

published March, 1881

This is another use of the title 'Over the Garden Wall'. This time it is used for a medley of songs from the repertoire of the Mohawk Minstrels, including titles such as 'Oh That My Love Were Near Me', 'Over the Garden Wall', 'Just Down the Lane', 'Under the Chestnut Tree', 'Happy with Thee, Love' and 'On the Banks of the Silvery Thames' mostly written by the Mohawk's chief lyricist Harry Hunter. The arranger was paid fifteen guineas for the absolute sale of all rights.

OVER THE GARDEN WALL
VALSE

ON POPULAR MELODIES
SELECTED & ARRANGED
BY

CHARLES GODFREY

B. M. ROYAL HORSE GUARDS.

FRANCIS BROS. & DAY, BLENHEIM HOUSE, OXFORD ST. W.

T. PACHER LITH.

STA. HALL

PRICE, ... 4/.
DUET, ... 4/.
SEPTETT, ... 1/.
FULL ORCHESTRA, ... 1/6
MILIT & BRASS COMBINED 3/6.

'THE SWEET LITTLE GIRL WITH THE JERSEY ON'

Music by Walter Redmond; lyrics by Harry Hunter;

sung by George Clare, the Mohawk Minstrels' Prima Donna;

published 1882

As the Mohawk Minstrels were an all-male group, carrying on the traditions of the earlier minstrel troupes, so the occasional female roles in the sketches and songs were performed by men such as George Clare, a member of the Mohawks in the 1880s. The Jersey of the title is a reference to a style of dress introduced by Jersey-born society beauty and actress Lillie Langtry (1852–1929). Known as the Jersey Lily, she was reputed to have been the mistress of Edward VII. In the song, the Jersey dress, which so clearly emphasizes the attributes of its wearer, attracts much admiration from attentive males, to the disapproval of older and no doubt plainer female relatives. The song's composer, Walter Redmond, was the Mohawk Minstrels' leading violinist.

THE SWEET LITTLE GIRL WITH THE JERSEY ON.

WRITTEN BY   COMPOSED BY

HARRY HUNTER. WALTER REDMOND.

SUNG WITH IMMENSE SUCCESS BY

MR. GEORGE CLARE.

THE MOHAWK MINSTRELS' PRIMA DONNA.

LONDON: FRANCIS BROTHERS & DAY, 351, OXFORD STREET, W.

ENT. STA. HALL.   Pr. 3/-

'SHOULDER TO SHOULDER'

Music by E. Jonghmans; lyrics by Harry Adams;

sung by Bessie Bonehill and by Grace Whiteford;

published October, 1882

Originally written as a patriotic song to stir up feelings of national pride at the beginning of the hostilities in Egypt in 1882, the words included such phrases as

The storm long brewing's burst at last

and

We've Beauchamp Seymour yet to show
What Englishmen can do

After the crushing defeat of Arabi Pasha at Tel-el-Kebir by the British forces under Sir Garnet Wolseley, a revised version of the song was quickly prepared:

The lines of Tel-ek-Kebir fell
And victory quickly came
Sir Garnet did his duty well
All honour to his name.

The mention of two artistes, Bessie Bonehill and Grace Whiteford, attests not only to the popularity of these self-congratulatory songs glorifying the might of Britannia, but also to the fact that they were often performed by women, usually dressed in male attire.

ALSO SUNG BY
MISS GRACE WHITEFORD

1697

SHOULDER TO SHOULDER

Price 3/-

SUNG WITH IMMENSE SUCCESS BY

MISS BESSIE BONEHILL,

WRITTEN BY
HARRY ADAMS.

COMPOSED BY
E. JONGHMANS.

FRANCIS BROS. & DAY, BLENHEIM HOUSE, OXFORD St. W.

T PACKER LITH

'RUN UP THE FLAG'

A patriotic song written by Clement Scott; music by Michael

Connelly; sung by Fannie Leslie;

published December, 1882

Fannie Leslie (1857–1935) called herself 'The Queen of Burlesque' and made a career on the musical stage and in variety as well as in music hall. She was married to theatre manager Walter Gooch, who presented her in a number of plays. She also appeared in musicals for George Edwardes at the famous Gaiety Theatre. In her music hall acts she usually performed as a male impersonator and sang 'masher' songs like Will Godwin's 'The Nineteenth Century Boys'. This patriotic song 'Run Up the Flag' is highly topical. It refers to specific army leaders in lines like:

The Cavalry did bravely by Lowe and Russell led,
But the army that took Egypt had Sir Garnet at its head.

This refers to Sir Garnet Wolseley and the British occupation of Egypt in 1882, but also contains a pointed reference to the resentment felt by some people for Queen Victoria's prolonged period of mourning for Prince Albert, and it calls for renewed loyalty and the suppression of republican sentiments. After calling for three cheers for the Army, three cheers for old England and one cheer more for Queen and Prince, it finishes with the lines:

So down with agitation that pulls the country down
The stalwart British nation stands on People and the Crown.

'BRITANNIA'S SONS'

Written, composed and sung by Joe Weatherhead;

published September, 1885

Throughout the heyday of the music hall, there was always a place for a stirring patriotic song extolling the virtues of the British armed forces. Although wars and military engagements in Africa and the remoter parts of the British Empire were certainly not unknown, the songs did not necessarily need a specific point of reference. This is an example of such a song that does nothing more than wave the flag, but there is no doubt that the music hall audiences of the day would have joined with enthusiasm and pride in the words of the chorus:

Shoulder arms! The bugle's sounding.
Beat the drum, beat the drum and let's away.
Britannia's sons with hearts rebounding
Still shall fight and win, hurrah!

BRITANNIA'S SONS,

OR

(THE DRUMMER IN THE COLDSTREAM GUARDS.)

STANNARD & SON.

WRITTEN, COMPOSED & SUNG

By

JOE. WEATHERHEAD.

ENT. STA. HALL.

Pr. 3/-

LONDON: FRANCIS BROS. & DAY, (BLENHEIM HOUSE) 195, OXFORD ST W.

PUBLISHERS OF SMALLWOOD'S PIANOFORTE TUTOR, THE EASIEST TO TEACH AND TO LEARN FROM.

2051.

'THE ARMY LANCERS'

Arranged by H.L. d'Arcy-Jaxone;

published 1889

The English novelist Rudyard Kipling (1865–1936) was immensely popular around the end of the nineteenth century and his series of poems about British Imperial India, 'Barrack Room Ballads', were particularly successful. Many of them were set to music by composers such as Gerard Cobb and Gordon Sutherland, and in this medley the titles include 'The Widow at Windsor', 'Mandalay', 'Fuzzy Wuzzy', 'Gunga Din', 'Danny Deever' and many more. The lancers was a particular form of quadrille with an elaborate fifth and final figure and was customarily based on existing songs or melodies from operas, whereas the quadrille was often specially composed.

THE · ARMY · LANCERS,

Simplified Edition.

17th Lancers.   Seaforth Highlanders.   10th Hussars.   Grenadier Guards.   Royal Irish Rifles.   2nd Life Guards.   Royal Welsh Fusiliers.

ngal Infantry.

GEO. TGE. LITH.

R. SIMKIN.

ARRANGED ON THE MELODIES OF THE CELEBRATED

BARRACK-ROOM BALLADS,

by

H. L. D'ARCY · JAXONE.

Price 4/=

LONDON, CHARLES SHEARD & Cº Music Publishers and Printers, 192 HIGH HOLBORN, W.C
The very latest issue of HEMY'S PIANOFORTE TUTOR is the SEYMOUR SMITH EDITION. ☞ BUY · NO · OTHER. ☜
BOSTON MASS. U.S.A. THE WHITE-SMITH Music Publishing Cº 62 & 64 STANHOPE STREET.

ght for all Countries

Orchestral Brass and Military Band Parts are Published by Messrs Lafleur & Son.

'FACING THE STORM'

Music by Warwick Williams; lyrics by Oswald Allan;
published 1887

This is not specifically a war song, despite the initial impression created by the cover design. It is a piece of propaganda directed against the 'Giant of Treason who stalks through the land' and 'the people who preach insurrection'; in reality a right-wing political attack on the activities of those people who were beginning to spread the ideas of Socialism. With the formation of the Fabian Society in 1884, some brilliant minds such as George Bernard Shaw and H.G. Wells had given intellectual support to these theories. At the same time the first practical results of the new dogmas were seen in the beginnings of the Labour Movement in Britain. The cover shows representatives of three different armed forces defending the Royal Standard, obviously meant to symbolize the monarch, in the struggle against the new revolutionary ideals that were beginning to gain support.

Facing the Storm.

(National Song.)

2321.

Written by OSWALD ALLAN. Composed by WARWICK WILLIAMS

Sung with Great Success in the London and Provincial Pantomimes.

Copyright.

Pr 3/-

LONDON;
FRANCIS BROS & DAY, (BLENHEIM HOUSE,) 195, OXFORD St W
PUBLISHERS OF
SMALLWOOD'S CELEBRATED PIANOFORTE TUTOR

'LES JOLIES FILLES'

Gavotte by Julian L'Estrange

This is a piano solo of a simple nature which could be played as a dance or as a salon piece. The cover is an example of a development in style whereby the lettering is an integral part of the design. In this case the ribbon of the hatbox, instead of being separately overlaid on the picture or completely outside it, is used to shape the words.

Les Jolies Filles

Gavotte

PAR

Julian L'Estrange.

W. Spalding delt

LONDON;
FRANCIS BROS & DAY, (BLENHEIM HOUSE,) 195, OXFORD ST W.
PUBLISHERS OF
SMALLWOOD'S CELEBRATED PIANOFORTE TUTOR.
Thos PACKER LITH.

Price, 4/-

2324.

Number Thirty

'BEAUX YEUX'

Valse by Stella Kappey

This is another example of the seemingly endless stream of easy piano solos published in the late Victorian era to cater to the demand for melodious but undemanding works for performance in the home.

DEDIÉE A LA COMTESSE. ADA KIELMANSEG.

BEAUX YEUX

STANNARD & SON.

"Les yeux noirs vont aux purgatoires,
Les yeux bleus vont aux cieux."

VALSE

BY

STELLA KAPPEY.

ENT STA HALL.

Pr. 4/.
SEPTETT . . . . . 1/.
FULL ORCHESTRA 1/6

LONDON: FRANCIS BROS. & DAY, (BLENHEIM HOUSE,) 195, OXFORD ST. W.
PUBLISHERS OF SMALLWOOD'S PIANOFORTE TUTOR, THE EASIEST TO TEACH & TO LEARN FROM.

'OH LET ME DREAM'

Music and lyrics by Ruth Boyd;

published 1910

Although by 1910 the beginnings of a new type of popular music, arising from ragtime and the negro-spiritual influence, were already being felt in the songs of the day, there were still many oldfashioned romantic ballads being produced of which this is a typical example. It is also curious that although the cover attributes the words to Ruth Boyd, the inside of the copy carries a credit for lyrics to Ballard MacDonald (1882–1935), a prolific writer whose hits included 'Play that Barbershop Chord' (1910, music by Lewis F. Muir), 'The Trail of the Lonesome Pine' (1913, music by Harry Carroll) and 'Back Home Again in Indiana' (1917, music by James F. Hanley).

'MABEL'

Music by P.D. de Coster; lyrics by Ren Shields; published 1910

In this catchy 1910 song, Mabel is a waitress who works at Childs, 'selling Java Beans and smiles'! The writer of the lyrics, Ren Shields, had already scored two huge hits with 'In the Good Old Summertime' (1902) and 'Waltz me Around Again, Willie' (1906) and in 1910 was to have another smash with 'Steamboat Bill'. The cover design is by Gene Buck (1885–1957), who was himself a well-known songwriter. Among his later hits was the engaging 1915 'telephone' song 'Hello Frisco' (music by Louis Hirsch), which enjoyed a revival in the 1943 film *Hello, Frisco, Hello* with Alice Faye. Gene Buck also directed on Broadway, mainly for the Ziegfeld Follies, and wrote songs with such distinguished composers as Jerome Kern and Victor Herbert. From 1924 to 1941 he was president of the American Society of Composers, Authors and Publishers (ASCAP).

MABEL

WORDS·BY
REN·SHIELDS

MUSIC·BY
P·D·DE·COSTER

GENE
BUCK

5 ·· JEROME·H·REMICK·&·C° NEW·YORK·DETROIT··

POPULAR·EDITION

'NOW SHE'S ANYBODY'S GIRLIE'

Music by Egbert Van Alstyne; lyrics by Harry Williams

Williams and Van Alstyne were a songwriting team whose most lasting creation was the 1905 romantic waltz 'In the Shade of the Old Apple Tree'. Van Alstyne was born in Illinois in 1882 and, after touring the West in vaudeville, he teamed up with Williams and the pair came to New York in 1900. The partnership had its first hit in 1903 with 'Navajo', which was the first popular song to make use of an American Indian name, and they followed it with another Indian title 'Cheyenne' in 1906. Also written by Williams and Van Alsytne in 1910 was 'Who Are You with Tonight?' In later years Van Alstyne went on to work with other writers, including Gus Kahn with whom he collaborated on the standards 'Memories' (1915) and 'Pretty Baby' (1916).

Now She's Anybody's Girlie

Song
by
WILLIAMS and
VAN ALSTYNE

5

Jerome H. Remick & Co.
New York   Detroit

'SOMETHING TO REMEMBER'

Music by John Conrad; lyrics by Gus Kahn;

published November, 1921

Gus Kahn (1886–1941) was one of the outstanding lyricists of American popular music in the first half of the twentieth century, writing for Hollywood and Broadway as well as Tin Pan Alley. After working with composers like Neil Moret, Richard Whiting and Egbert Van Alstyne, Kahn joined forces with Walter Donaldson (1893–1947) during the twenties. They were to write some memorable songs including 'My Buddy', 'Carolina in the Morning', 'Love Me or Leave Me' and 'Yes Sir, that's My Baby' as well as scores for shows and films like *Whoopee* and *Kid Millions*, both starring Eddie Cantor. Kahn also continued to write with other composers besides Donaldson, and in 1924 he had no less than three big hits with music by the band leader Isham Jones (1894–1956), namely 'Spain', 'I'll see You in My Dreams' and 'It Had to be You', all of which enjoyed substantial revivals in the 1940s. Other Kahn songs include 'Toot Toot Tootsie' (with Erdman and Russo), 'Liza' (with Ira and George Gershwin) and the songs for the first Fred Astaire and Ginger Rogers film *Flying Down to Rio* (1933) with music by Vincent Youmans (1898–1946), including 'Orchids in the Moonlight' and 'The Carioca'.

OPERATIC EDITION

Something to Remember

Song

LYRIC BY
GUS KAHN
MUSIC BY
JOHN CONRAD

MADE IN U·S·A·

JEROME H. REMICK & CO
NEW YORK   DETROIT

'WHO BELIEVED IN YOU?'

Music by Anatol Friedland; lyrics by L. Wolfe Gilbert;

published September, 1921

Anatol Friedland (1881–1938) was born in Russia in St Petersburg and studied music at the Moscow Conservatory. After coming to the USA he studied architecture at Columbia University, but continued his musical activities by running the Club Anatol in New York in the 1920s. He also wrote popular songs including 'Are You from Heaven', 'Shades of the Night', and 'Singapore', all with lyrics by L. Wolfe Gilbert whose collaborations with other writers had already produced such successes as 'Hitchy Koo' and the quintessential ragtime song 'Waiting for the Robert E. Lee', both dating from 1912. The best product of the Friedland-Gilbert partnership was the deliberately absurd song 'Lily of the Valley' (1917), which made a reappearance in the 1947 Betty Grable film *Mother Wore Tights.*

WHO
(BELIEVED IN YOU?)

by
Anatol Friedland

Published by
ANATOL FRIEDLAND
903 PALACE THEATRE BLDG
NEW YORK

_____

'SAYONARA'

Intermezzo by Neil Moret;
published 1923

This is an instrumental piece on the eternal theme of farewell by Charles N. Daniels who wrote under the pseudonym of Neil Moret. As well as other instrumental numbers like 'Hiawatha' (1901) and 'Silverheels' (1905), Moret collaborated on some extremely successful and enduring songs including 'On Mobile Bay' (1910, words by Earle C. Jones), 'You Tell Me Your Dream' (1908, words by Seymour A. Rice and Al H. Brown; later, new words were added by Gus Kahn when the original writers failed to renew their copyright), 'Chloe' (1927, words by Gus Kahn) and 'Moonlight and Roses' (1925, words by Ben Black). This last song was based on the smoothly flowing 'Andantino' for organ by Edwin Lemare. Another interesting song by Neil Moret with words by Harry Williams is 'Mickey', written in 1918 as a direct tie-up with Mack Sennett's silent movie of the same name, starring Mabel Normand to whom the song is 'respectifully' dedicated. 'Mickey' had a strong revival in 1947, with a million-seller record for Ted Weems.

SAYONARA

INTERMEZZO·
BY
NEIL·MORET

JEROME H REMICK & C°
NEW·YORK··DETROIT

POPULAR·EDITION

'THE PARISIENNE WALK'

Music by Herman Paley; lyrics by Nat Vincent; published simultaneously in the USA and the UK on 18 September, 1916

Typical of so many dance songs of the time, this 1916 composition describes itself as 'a brand new dance sensation' and 'the craze of the day'. It is in fact just one in a very long line of such songs which satisfied the apparently endless demand for new dances which had begun in the USA soon after the turn of the century and which was part of the birth of what might be called pop music. The rhythms were developed from the original ragtime music of composers like Scott Joplin and Joseph Lamb with characteristics of the negro dances such as the cake-walk. Early examples of the popular songs which formed part of the development of the dance craze were Harry von Tilzer's 'Cubanola Glide' (1909), George Botsford's 'Grizzly Bear' (1910) and Louis Hirsch's 'Gaby Glide' (1911). The craze continued unabated throughout the First World War and most of the musical shows of the time contained one or even more new dances such as 'The Tickle Toe' in Louis Hirsch's *Going Up* of 1918, and 'The Ring-a-Ling' *and* 'The Kipling Walk' in Nat Ayer's 1916 revue *The Bing Boys are Her*.
The one 'new' dance from this procession of Bunny Hugs, Turkey Trots and other animal gyrations to survive to this day is the Foxtrot. It first appeared in songs like 'My Fox Trot Girl' in 1907 but became fully established at the peak of the dance craze era around 1914 in the performances of the professional dancing couples who had begun to appear in stage shows and ballrooms led by the famous Irene and Vernon Castle. The lyricist Nat Vincent was a vaudeville artist with a talent for songwriting. He is responsible in part for the creation of 'I'm Forever Blowing Bubbles' (1918) which is today sung by the supporters of London's West Ham football team.

THE PARISIENNE WALK

SONG

LYRIC BY
NAT VINCENT

MUSIC BY
HERMAN PALEY

5

JEROME H. REMICK & CO.
NEW YORK   DETROIT

'PEACOCK STRUT'

Foxtrot by 'Friscoe' and Martyn;
published 1917

This is an example of an instrumental piece, written in 1917, in response to the never-ending demand for popular new dance music, which had already worked its way through much of the animal kingdom with 'The Grizzly Bear' (1910), 'The Leg of Mutton' (1913), 'The Bunny Hug'. It took in the birds of the sky and land with 'The Turkey Trot' (1912), 'The Pigeon Walk' (1914), 'The Eagle Rock', and everything else besides in 'The Texas Tommy Dance' (1913), 'Ballin' the Jack' (1913), 'Kerry Mills Cake Walk' (1915) and even something called the 'Shim-Me-Sha-Wabble' in 1915.

POPULAR EDITION
PEACOCK STRUT
FOX-TROT
BY
"FRISCOE" AND MARTYN
NEW YORK

Number Thirty-Nine

'FIMMEL-FOX'

Music by Hugo Hirsch;
published 1921

This is a German composition in the tradition of the many 'animal' dances that were written during the early part of the present century. The title uses the slang word 'Fimmel' which means 'Crazy' and links it to what was to be the most enduring of all the animal-based dances, the Foxtrot. The composer Hugo Hirsch was born in Birnbaum in 1884 but between 1933 and 1950 lived in London and Paris. In 1950 he returned to Berlin where he died in 1961. His compositions included popular songs, operettas and film scores.

'DU HAST MICH TOLL GEMACHT'

Music by Ernst Steffan; lyrics by Arthur Rebner;
published 1922

Born in 1890 in Vienna, Ernst Steffan was a child prodigy who began as a concert pianist but later became a conductor and composer. In addition to his popular songs, he wrote a number of operettas including *Betty* (1914), *Das Milliarden Souper* (1921) and *Munchausen* (1927). He died in Berlin in 1967. Arthur Rebner was born in Lemberg in 1890. After working as a composer and lyricist for some years in Vienna, he went to France in 1938 and eventually settled in Los Angeles, where he died in 1949.

'EINMAL'

Music by Ernst Steffan; lyrics by Arthur Rebner; published 1922

This is another popular song from the team of Rebner and Steffan, who wrote a number of successful songs together in the early 1920s. The design by Herzig is typical of the style of German music covers of the time and captures the spirit of the combination of sophistication and decadence with which Berlin became synonymous between the two world wars.

'ICH SCHENK' DIR DAS HERZ EINER ROSE'

Music and lyrics by Robert Katscher;
published 1929

Robert Katscher was born in Vienna in 1894 and attained a degree in law as well as studying musical composition with the Austrian musicologist and composer, Hans Gal. He wrote a number of Viennese songs, film scores and operettas, including *Die Wunderbar* and *Essig und Öl*. His song 'Madonna', published in Vienna in 1924, was given a set of English lyrics by Buddy de Sylva and was published in 1926 in the USA as 'When Day is Done'. It became a major hit and has remained a standard ever since. Katscher died in Hollywood in 1942.

Ich schenk' Dir das Herz einer Rose...

LIED UND ENGLISH WALTZ.

Text und Musik
von
Robert Katscher.

WIENER BOHEME
VERLAG
(Otto Hein.)
ZENTRALE: ZWEIGSTELLE:
Wien, IV.,   ★   Berlin W 15.
Rechte Wienzeile 33.   Brandenburgische Str. 27

'ZWEI BLAÜE AÜGEN'

Music by Hans May; lyrics by Richard Rillo;
published 1930

The name Hans May was a pseudonym used by the composer Johann Mayer, who was born in Vienna in 1886 and died in London in 1958. He wrote the songs for a number of German films starring the very popular tenor Joseph Schmidt. They included 'Ein Lied geht am die Welt' (1933), which also achieved success in an English version 'My Song Goes Round the World' with lyrics by Jimmy Kennedy, and 'Ein Stern fallt von Himmel' (1934), which was also a hit in its English version, 'A Star Fell from Heaven', published in 1936 with new words by Ruth Feiner. After moving to England in the mid-1930s, Mayer continued to write the scores for a large number of British films, such as Carol Reed's *The Stars Look Down* (1940), *Madonna of the Seven Moons* (1945) and *The Wicked Lady* (1946). In 1954 he had a big success with London's West End musical *Wedding in Paris* (lyrics by Sonny Miller), starring Evelyn Laye.

'ZWEI TRÄNEN . . .'

Music by Rubens and Franz Grothe; lyrics by Fritz Rotter;
published 1930

The composer Franz Grothe was born in Berlin in September 1908 and died in Cologne in 1981. His range of musical activities encompassed the writing of songs, symphonic jazz and operettas, as well as arranging the scores for operettas by other composers. Grothe was for many years the conductor of the German Radio Orchestra in Berlin. He also contributed musical scores to many major German films, especially for the singing stars Marta Eggerth (*Die blonde Carmen, Immer wenn ich glücklich bin* and *Ihr grösster Erfolg*), Marika Rökk (*Frauen sind doch bessere Diplomaten, Der Tanz mit dem Kaiser* and the first German colour film *Die Frau meiner Träume*), and Erna Berger, the opera singer who supplied the voice for Ilse Werner in the film *The Swedish Nightingale*. For 'Zwei tränen' Grothe collaborated with a Russian composer, Leo Goltzmann, who was born in Kiev in 1897. Goltzmann emigrated to Paris where he spent most of his time as a violinist and conductor, but also wrote music under the various pseudonyms of Bela Dajos, Eddi Thommsen and Eddi Rubens.

Zwei Tränen...

Verse von
Fritz Rotter

Lied und Tango.

Musik von
Rubens
und
Franz Grothe

WIENER BOHEME
VERLAG
(Otto Hein.)

ZENTRALE·   ·ZWEIGSTELLE·
Wien. IV.,   Berlin W 15.
Rechte Wienzeile 33.   Brandenburgische Str 27

'WAS MACHT JEDE NACHT SO EIN KLEINES BABY IN DER BAR?'

Music and lyrics by Fritz Rotter and Dr B. Kaper;

published 1930

This is a song by two writers who later both moved to Hollywood, during the 1930s, and there achieved separate success. Fritz Rotter was born in Vienna in 1900, but his early career was based in Berlin where he wrote many songs for revues and films, including material for Marta Eggerth and Richard Tauber. In Hollywood he continued to work on film songs and produced titles such as 'Take Me in Your Arms' with Mitchell Parish in 1943 and 'Spring Came Back to Vienna', which was sung by Jane Powell in MGM's 1948 hit *Luxury Liner*. Bronislau Kaper was born in Warshau in 1902 and after working in Germany he settled in Hollywood in 1934; his first big success was the song 'San Francisco', written with Gus Kahn and Walter Jurmann for the 1936 film of the same name, starring Clark Gable and Jeanette MacDonald. Before that he had already written 'Cosi cosa' for Alan Jones in the 1935 Marx Brothers film *A Night at the Opera*, and he later provided songs for some of the screen's biggest singing stars, including Deanna Durbin and Kathryn Grayson. In 1953 he had a tremendous success with the music for *Lili*, starring Leslie Caron, from which the hit song 'Hi Lili, Hi Lo' with words by Helen Deutsch was a chart topper.

'WANN SPRECHEN WIR VON LIEBE?'

Music by Ludwig Friedmann; lyrics by Fritz Rotter;

published 1929

The composer Ludwig Friedmann was born in Berlin in 1875 and died there in 1933 after a successful career as writer of many popular songs and some operettas. He was one of the directors of the 'Drei Masken' music publishing company.

'KÜSS MICH NICHT AUF DEN MUND'

Music by Richard Fall; lyrics by Arthur Rebner;

published 1930

Richard Fall was born in 1882 in Sewitsch in what is now Czechoslovakia. His compositions included operettas as well as film scores and popular hits. His father was a military bandmaster who also did some composing, and his brothers Siegfried and Leo were also professional musicians. Leo became internationally famous as the composer of operettas such as *The Dollar Princess*, *Die geschiedene Frau* (staged in London as *The Girl in the Train*) and *Madame Pompadour*.

'GNÄDIGSTE, SIE BRAUCHEN EINEN FREUND'

Music by Willy Engel-Berger; lyrics by Erwin W. Spahn; published 1929

Wilhelm Engel-Berger was born in Bonn in 1890, the son of a prosperous merchant. Instead of going into the family business as was expected of him, the young man studied music with a view to concentrating on symphonic and church music. With the money he inherited after his father's death he formed a band and sailed around the world four times with the Hamburg-America shipping line. His phenomenal memory and gift for improvisation enabled him to play the national music of all the passengers, including Arabian, Persian and Indian. Later he worked with Willy Schäffer in Berlin and as a bar-pianist in Vienna where in 1946 he wrote the music for the first post-war Austrian film *Der weite Weg*. At that time he intended to enter the monastery of an Armenian order in Vienna because Armenian sacred music had made a deep impression on him during his travels. Unfortunately, he did not live to do so as he died in Vienna in 1946 after a short period of mental illness.

'EIN BISCHEN SEIDE – UND DARIN DU!'

Music by Willy Engel-Berger; lyrics by Wilhelm Sterk;
published 1929

By 1929 the Foxtrot and Slow Foxtrot had established themselves as the most common form for popular songs, especially for subjects of a romantic nature. This song, which translates as 'A Little Bit of Silk – with You Inside!', is typical of the mildly erotic popular songs that were current in Germany and Austria in the 1920s, as also exemplified by the other Continental items in this collection.

'L'INCONNU'

Music by Jean Lenoir; lyrics by Darny;
published 1925

This is the only example in the present collection of a French music cover, but it is clearly in the same style as the foregoing German and Austrian designs and the girl has the unmistakable features that are so closely associated with the 1920s.

L'iNCONNU...

Prix : 4 fr.

PAROLES de
DARNY
MUSIQUE de
JEAN LENOIR

 ÉDITION ARLEQUIN

10, Rue des Petits-Carreaux, PARIS (2ᵉ)